Edgar Fawcett

Romance and Revery

Poems

Edgar Fawcett

Romance and Revery
Poems

ISBN/EAN: 9783743328556

Manufactured in Europe, USA, Canada, Australia, Japa

Cover: Foto ©Andreas Hilbeck / pixelio.de

Manufactured and distributed by brebook publishing software
(www.brebook.com)

Edgar Fawcett

Romance and Revery

ROMANCE AND REVERY

POEMS

By EDGAR FAWCETT

To my Friend,

WILLIAM HENRY RIDEING,

IN MEMORY OF HAPPY DAYS

BOTH HERE AND ABROAD,

This Book

IS AFFECTIONATELY INSCRIBED.

CONTENTS.

iv CONTENTS.

CONTENTS.

ROMANCE AND REVERY.

THE MAGIC FLOWER.

DEEP in a land of heavy-foliaged heights,
    Clear-cloven of one fair lordly river, stood
A palace made for manifold delights
    And compassed by a noble-towering wood.
Here lived (how anciently were hard to tell)
A king whom all his people honored well.

And years before that time his worshipped wife,
    A queen Madonna-browed and saintly-eyed,
With anguish had surrendered life for life,
    But momently a mother ere she died;
And now within these palace-walls dwelt one,
A princess, with long tresses like the sun.

Ethereal in her symmetry, and tall,
    And graceful as a lily when breeze-bent,
She moved among her maidens, over all
    Supreme for dignity and sweetness blent,
With neither costly robe nor jewel rare
To match the marvels of her eyes and hair.

Some influence from her mother's watchful soul
    Inseparably round the Princess breathed,
And seemed, at times, a shadowy aureole
    Among her glimmering tresses faintly wreathed;
And it was told that where she slept by night
A Presence watched her, made from misty light!

Her countenance no woodland creature saw
    But straightway, on that instant, it became
Obedient to some mysterious law,
    And followed if she called it, meekly tame;
And rose-vines round an oriel in her room
Were bright with fadeless fealty of bloom!

Now the good King, her father, having thought
    How wondrously his child was pure and fair,
Desponded that the drift of fate had brought
    His throne the blessing of no lineal heir;
For in this land whereof he held the throne,
No woman might aspire to reign alone.

But he to whom a princess gave her hand
 When brotherless and born the eldest, might
(So ran the old sacred statutes of the land)
 Reign monarch by indisputable right.
And meditating that his death drew near,
The King was smitten with a grievous fear.

" For who among our courtiers noblest-born
 Deserves," he mused, "to wed this matchless maid?
Lo! is it frivolous Rolf, whom gems adorn?
 Or stripling Bertram, of the spleenful blade?
Or Ronald, of the ringlets? or, yet worse,
Young black-browed Otho, of the gamester's purse?

" Ah, none of these! And surely on our realm
 Are fallen most evil days! True men no more,
Guileless of heart, invincible of helm,
 Prop the proud throne with counsel, as of yore!
That mightier-limbed and lofty-thoughted race
Has past, and weak successors hold its place.

" Gentle, heroic, temperate, simply great,
 Were those of whom our treasured legends tell, —
Columnar spirits, on whose strength our state
 Was builded and upborne, whate'er befell!
Calm fortresses, round whose repose and pride
The assailant waves of discord broke and died!

" But now what mockeries meet and taunt me here!
    How shattered are this people that I rule!
How airily grave statecraft lends an ear
    To jinglings of the bell-besprinkled fool!
How lighter than its wearer's giddy sports
The gay plume flashes in my fountained courts!"

Thus musing, from his casement glanced the King
    Where monstrous oaks o'ershadowed a green lawn
Dappled with sunbeams richly flickering,
    And there, serene beside a star-eyed fawn,
He marked his child, — a shape of virgin grace,
Standing white-vestured in that cloistral place.

"Daughter whom I so cherish," thought the sire,
    " Sweet living semblance of thy mother dead,
What man, however princely, ought aspire
    To share my great crown with thy hallowed head?
Better than mateless marriage for thy doom,
Death's kisses and the bride-bed of the tomb!" . . .

Later by some few days, throughout the land
    A loudening rumor passed; and these who heard
Were credulous of what the King had planned,
    But those disdainfully believed no word;
And lastly, while men trusted or denied,
The voice of proclamation sounded wide.

And thus it spoke: " *To all the truth is known,*
  So often in song or story sung or told,
Of how for many a century has blown
  In some high fastness or deep-tangled wold
Of these wide-looming hills that round us tower,
The hidden splendors of a Magic Flower.

" *Yet no man breathes to-day whose eyes have seen*
  The covert where its mystic charms endure;
And through past ages it has only been
  A vision for the marvellously pure.
And if the seeker's life wear spot or stain,
Though for a life he seek, he shall not gain.

" *So radiant this enchanted Flower, it seems*
  A fair star fallen upon the earth's dull breast!
For dying searchers of old time in dreams
  Beheld it after years of empty quest;
But even who truly saw, in that far day,
Lacked the white sinlessness to bear away.

" *Now, therefore, doth the reigning King proclaim*
  That if within his ample realm be one
(Whether of lofty lineage and proud name,
  Or lowliest of all men beneath the sun)
Who brings the famed Flower to the palace-gate,
Him doth a princess and a throne await."

So heralded, the royal message ran;
   And wonder filled the people, and for days
No man throughout the realm encountered man
   But each his judgment spoke, with eager phrase:
And all believed for surety, worst and best,
He lived not who might venture on the quest.

But they whose pleasure was in careless thought,
   And flippant speech, and fashion's random aims,
And robes of price fantastically wrought,
   And railleries among the beauteous dames, —
These gentry of the palace, when they heard,
Grew merry, jesting with the royal word.

And where, with purple, gold or scarlet dress,
   Down vistas that the elm and oak made dark,
In luxury, in languor and idlesse,
   Gallant and lady roamed the leafy park,
Such lightsome scoffs were on the lips of these
That peals of ringing laughter pierced the trees.

" Poor trustful King! " compassionated they,
   Mirth cheapening the pity of their tone;
" He dreams, forsooth, to-day is yesterday,
   Unmindful that the world is older grown
And far more wise than, taking false for true,
Wills-o'-the-wisp whole lifetimes to pursue! "

Thus jeeringly they spoke; but neither King
   Nor Princess heard an echo of their jeers.
Yet one, a simple vassal, hearkening,
   His pain had fitly told with sighs and tears,
Because there dwelt within his patient breast
Much reverential honor of the quest.

But latterly these pomps of court he knew,
   Brought thither by a selfish kinsman old,
Who from plebeian life had risen, and who
   Willed that to none their kinship should be told;
Since he, the King's High Steward, ill could bear
Such blood as this poor serving-lad's to share.

And yet, though hardened, like so many lives
   Girt constantly with jars of warring needs, —
Where this man hilt to hilt with that man strives
   And heartless comment hails the first who bleeds, —
Though grasping, worldly, ruthless, he had made
The vow for which his dying sister prayed.

To guard her orphan son had been that vow, —
   Thus far but lightly kept, if kept in truth;
For seldom save at secret meeting, now,
   He looked with heedful glance upon the youth,
Nor noted then, so slight and cold his care,
Deep eyes and shapely frame and modest air.

Nor did he dream that in a month's brief space
 Among all fellow-servitors had grown
Love for the lad's mild manners and calm face
 And culture of sweet speech unlike their own;
How even the rudest in his sight felt shame,
And strangely coarseness was not where he came.

Though sprung in truth from parentage obscure,
 Since boyhood he had far excelled his kind,
Having a soul pre-eminently pure,
 A glowing faith, a large and limpid mind,
A heart unsoiled of envies, greeds or hates,
Lifted in loveliness above its mates!

Yet none than he with humbler spirit bore
 The part 't was fortune's pleasure to assign,
Waiting in chamber and in corridor,
 Serving at feast the garnet-colored wine;
Standing at throne-foot on grand audience-days,
Immovable below the crown's rich blaze.

High in the highest of those palace-towers
 His room was reared, aloof from passers' heed;
And here at morning or at midnight hours
 Greatly it pleasured him to muse and read,
Above the dense trees bowering the broad lawns,
Up near the wan stars or the damask dawns!

Released one midnight from the festal shine
   Where courtiers revelled late with noisy zest,
By many a coil of stairway serpentine
   At last he reached the chamber of his rest,
And found the placid place with moonbeams lit,
As though dead lilies' souls were haunting it.

O'er all the meagre plainness of the room
   A spell of soft aerial silver reigned;
But bold there gleamed from out its dubious gloom
   A griffon-crested casement, mullion-paned.
And he drew slowly near the casement's edge,
Leaning an arm upon the stony ledge.

Cloudless above him vastly curved the night,
   Where deep on deep of glowing heaven was laid;
Below, the illumined river with its light
   Pierced the remote solemnities of shade,
As though the lands, for many a meadowed mile,
Parted their dark lips in one dazzling smile!

Broad open soon he flung the casement-panes,
   And felt the breezes hurrying cool and fleet,
Sweet as fresh waters to his fevered veins,
   To brow and eyelids delicately sweet,
Breathe of their distant native hills that rose,
In monumental vagueness of repose.

And now aloft he raised both eager arms,
   While on his face the summer moon fell fair,
Showing it sad for sorrow such as harms
   More deeply by despondence than despair; . . .
Then suddenly, before his lifted sight,
A meteor dropt along the monstrous night.

" Perchance," he murmured, "'as an omen sent,
   This wild star, fading on the sky's blue scope,
May symbol mockery and disheartenment
   To my presumptuous and insensate hope!
The great hills call me with air-whispers cool . . .
Heaven answers from disdainful heights: ' Thou fool!'

" Ah! what is my poor trivial aim to theirs,
   The aspirant souls that strongly strove and died,
Guerdonless after many toilful cares,
   With effort ceaselessly unsatisfied?
Brave souls, like meteors, in audacious flight
Breaking their hearts of fire along the night!

"These fought and failed. . . . Shall I not fail as they?
   Though victory's hidden paradise be sweet,
In vain for centuries might the searcher stray,
   To grope through dizzying vistas of defeat!
Ah! no; the better lives thus vainly spent,
Crush courage with their weight of precedent!"

And now he turned, those dreary words being said,
  And many times along the chamber dim
Paced with close-folded arms, with low-drooped head,
  Doubt and belief at bitter war in him;
And ever while he paced, the fluttering air
Played in long tender waftures through his hair

An hour so fled, and at its end he stood
  Again beside the casement, and had now
Grown from tumultuous into grave of mood,
  With record of resolve on lips and brow.
And presently the voice wherewith he spoke
Depths of sweet-sounding earnestness awoke:

" In vain, dead searchers, ye have never died!
  Your failure wears the glory of success!
Better in great things to have greatly tried
  Than loftily to have achieved in less!
Low ye are fallen, and yet your fame shall dwell
Proud as the fearless distances ye fell!

" Of waves that buffet some bold steep of stone,
  Not those which round the rigid bases curl
Would fitly meet it, but that wave alone
  Which climbs to perish in a mist of pearl!
Though while it dies the sea-bird mocks its roar,
Ocean is glad of it from shore to shore!

" Be mine the effort, though the fall be mine,
　And never it is given my feet to near
The fairy fastness where that bloom divine
　Stars its still solitude from year to year!
I shall go forth ere warbles the first lark
And morning murmurs through the palace-park!

" I shall go forth, on hope's glad mission bound,
　Heedless though I be journeying to despair;
As, while deep-plunged within some cave profound,
　Some torch-flame to the last will crimson air!
So, till despair's black void shall bid it fade,
Hope shall be hope, unquenched and undismayed!

" And ah! hope-strengthening, there shall still abide
　The fervor of that dream which late has grown
A shadow-like attendance at my side,
　Wed to my life as to a flute its tone!
O thou, pure perfectly, above all blame,
Even thought bows reverence to name thy name!

" What wonder if the wild quest that I dare,
　Look promise-laden after those dull days
In which with calm and silence I would bear
　The unhappy doom no utterance could phrase? —
Her my poor creatureship so high above
Loving with love that was so rashly love!

" Oft have I climbed to this room's lonesome height
  And wept hot tears that I would shame to weep,
Striving across my soul's clear-seen delight
  To draw the obscuring drapery of sleep,
As one might rise and make his window dim,
Wakeful for some low gold moon watching him.

" Yet all my patient strivings were as naught,
  And not again the old peace was ever won,
And always to its lofty love my thought
  Staid loyal as the sunflower to its sun :
While she, that knew not of this woful thrall,
Knew not moreover if I was at all !

" Then came at last my golden day of days !
  Her yearly birth-feast gleamed with royal wealth ;
I, kneeling low beneath her maiden gaze
  While the great King and courtiers pledged her health,
Proffered the jewelled cup she leaned and took,
Blessing me while she leaned with one bright look !

'A moment, and her sweet eyes turned from mine,
  Claimed of subservient throngs on either hand ;
But in my veins the glad blood leapt like wine,
  And amorous music made the air turn bland,
While through the music borne, a vague voice said :
' For that she knows thou art, be comforted ! '

" Always thenceforward, wheresoe'er we met,
　　I found some slight sign on her face that told
How yet I was remembered, and how yet
　　The precious memory had not waxen cold;
But on bare sward gleams April's earliest kiss
Not faintlier than the smile that told me this!

" And now I seemed as one whose joyful sight
　　Sees lines of dull and beetling cliff disclose
Reaches of pasture, affluent with light,
　　Wooded and watered for a god's repose, —
Though, while within his breast desire burns hot,
'T is fate that valleyward he wander not!

" Still, sight is given for rapture. . . . So, akin,
　　Knowledge that now seemed knowledge, now surmise,
Made it not all mere misery to have been,
　　Filled life not wholly with dissentient sighs.
Dark frowned the crags; but dells whence odors came,
Busied their bird-throats with my carolled name!

" No longer was it strange that I grew bold,
　　Believing much and fondly fancying more,
My days to one rich dreamy cadence rolled,
　　'She loves thee!''loves thee!' 'loves thee!' o'er and o'er .
No longer was it strange that passion strong
Sundered restraint and blossomed into song!

" Dropt on that shadowed path which bough and bole
    Picture at ending with a reach of sky,
Where always 't is her evening wish to stroll
    Companionless, I let these poor words lie,
Known but for color from some oak's fallen leaf,
And yet no lightlier touched with tints of grief :

" ' *If flowers have been that never saw the sun,*
    Or birds, fleet-plumed, that never voyaged air,
Or well-wrought lutes, unplayed by any one,
    Or faultless women that no man called fair ;
If these things ever have been, my heart brings
A hopeless dream, to match it with these things !

" ' *Even as a corpse, my dream, with shrouded face,*
    Is borne where no light falls, no breeze may stir,
Is borne in sorrowing silence to the place
    Of cold serene eternal sepulchre !
Lift not the enfolding cerements, lest thou weep,
Moved by the pathos of its marble sleep !

" ' *For since on thy pure life no blame should rest,*
    Because thou wert but worshipped from afar
With longing such as when the sea's prone breast
    Throbs incommunicably to some star,
Surely that thou shouldst mourn my dream when dead,
Nothing hereafter shall have profited ! '

"Thus plaintive ran the song that I had wrought;
  And watchful of the dim path where it lay,
I lingered on till cool-aired evening brought
  The Princess, gliding in her graceful way:
Unseen I lingered, and unseen erelong
I saw her white hand hovering o'er the song.

"But straightway then I felt quick terror draw
  Thrill after thrill from faltering heart to brain,
And strangely, as with altered vision, saw
  This, my late act, rash, insolent and vain;
Then fled, like one whom some sharp wound provokes,
Fleet-footed through the labyrinthine oaks.

"With poignance of unspeakable regret
  For folly such as wakened wisdom shows,
Tireless amid the hours until we met,
  Self-accusation dealt its deadly blows;
And on the morrow my wrung spirit knew
How night's black prophecies were proven true!

"For even as one who loves a wild-wood place
  Because of leafy charms he has often seen,
Yet misses now a well-remembered grace
  Wind-ravaged from its garlandries of green;
So, passing her, I marked the clear eyes grown
To one calm blank avoidance of my own.

" All beauty engirt her sweetly, as of old;
   But now no dear regardful gleam was lent
To light, in their smooth harmony of mould,
   Unsullied brow or classic lineament.
And morrow, lapsing into morrow, bare
Fresh fagots to the flame of my despair!

" For since my love had ventured from the first
   No height of hope more daring than to show
The unspoken curse wherewith its life was curst,
   The knowledge of that joy 't was death to know,
Meaning not bolder by the song's late strain
Than when some wearied captive moves his chain;

" Since I the lowliest part had willed to play,
   And homage not unseemlier to allege
Than those rich flowers that bloom in bright array
   Perpetually round her casement's edge,
Thrilling, I doubt not, through each burdened stem
If her benignant eyes approve of them, —

" Now, therefore, that I sought this mediate sense
   Between cold vassalage and love's warm phrase,
Yet proffered but a menial's insolence,
   Jeered from the encircling world on all my days!
The brutes, the flowers, earth, water, sky or air
Had right of reverence that I could not share!

" And so in drear disquietude I past
    Through hours of darkness whose appointed end
Seemed possible alone when death at last
    The shade of its austerer gloom should send, —
Till that strange message, loud along the land,
Cheered like the waving of a far white hand !

" Lo, now the patriarch King proclaims ! and lo,
    Disloyalty contemns his high decree !
Yet on the wild quest men refuse I go, —
    I go, nor shall much toil dishearten me !
Hide well, strange haughty Flower, that wondrous crest !
Another life is arming for thy quest !

" Powers of the darkness, Powers of the wind or light,
    Mysterious, masterful, whate'er ye are
That shroud this peerless bloom from mortal sight
    As black-winged thunder shrouds a sparkling star,
Does now, while mountainward my words are borne,
Scorn on dim awful faces answer scorn ?

" In some still cavern, sacred to your spells,
    Group ye, with knit brows and strong folded arms,
The resolute unpitying sentinels
    Whom this my purpose grieves not nor alarms ?
Or do ye sigh that one more life should spend
Bright-blooded youth toward an empty end ?

" Spirits, I may not know if pity fills
   Your hearts with lenient heed of my heart's woe;
Or if ye keep alike for all men's ills
   Unvarying scorn, Spirits, I may not know!
But whether hate or whether love be yours,
Be mine the zeal that till I die endures!" . . .

Thus having murmured, ere an hour he stood
   Where moon-made arabesques lay sweet to see
Under the breezy leafage of that wood
   Which reared on all sides many a massive tree;
Nor lingered long, but fared till far away
The royal towers loomed huge in breaking day.

Before him, at the horizon, waved the clear
   Bough-vestured contour of those hills he sought,
Here broken with meadowy intervals, and here
   In spaces of long shadowy forest wrought,
Their summits turbaned with pale misty fleece,
Dawn-flushed and plastic to the wind's caprice.

Now on toward those majestic hills he bore;
   And just at noon he knelt beside a spring
Set like a jewel in a glade's green floor,
   And drank, and heard the mavis carolling,
Or close at hand the rich euphonious boom
Of wild bees revelling in a brake of bloom.

And now it seemed that all sweet sounds or sights
  Were touched with pensiveness in tone or hue,
Here at the land-rim whence those wooded heights
  Billowed immense against the northern blue;
From sky-tint, bird-song, leaf-gloss or wind-swell
Farewell reiterating soft farewell!

For he had gained that limit whence began
  Perchance the unchanging doom of keen unrest. . . .
And here the annalist would vainly scan
  By separate episodes his patient quest,
Since each day's fresh toil brought, in weary way,
Laborious likeness to its yesterday.

And time went flowing along, but he was now
  A wanderer still, his stubborn hope not dead,
Wearing maturer signs on cheek and brow,
  Bounteously bearded and wild-garmented;
Older by years, and yet with youth well seen
In stalwart stature and in virile mien.

No constant home for night or day was his;
  With none to heed where he might pause, whence flit
His life was even as some fleet mute life is,
  Ignorant that its own shade follows it;
And ever, where he staid to sleep, the spot
Through all its myriad morrows knew him not.

For drink the mountain streams gave crystal store,
  The foliaged wildernesses gave for food
Snared game, and berries that its bushes bore,
  And many a savage herb or root-growth rude;
And the steep lands he roamed for slumber gave
Countless complexities of pass and cave.

Nor through those lands did winter work large ill:
  Snows came not, or fell lightly if they fell;
Whence in all seasons he might search at will
  Summit by summit or deep dell by dell;
And wherefore seldom was he doomed to dare
The wilder savageries of earth and air.

Sandalled he was in strong-thonged rugged wise,
  And clothed with sturdy skins of his own spoil,
Flexile the girth of shoulder and of thighs
  To raiment fitly for his mountain toil, —
Seeming, apparelled thus, a shape that trod
Guardian of those acclivities and god!

But mercilessly glided on the years,
  And yet the elusive guerdon was not gained;
And moods possessed him now of lonely tears,
  Like blood-drops from his heart's hot centre drained;
And age, that spares no mortal strength of limb,
Became as unseen shackles clasping him.

Then, while hope withered in his wearied breast,
   And his dead youth a phantom summons grew,
Valleyward luring him, since life at best
   Of unborn days held meagre residue,
Still he staid firm, and with unfailing will
Wrought him a staff, and weakly wandered still.

" For now," he mused, " the end is near and sure;
   The story of my long quest is all but told;
My life, a tremulous leaf, hangs insecure;
   Death's wind is fluttering round its languid hold.
Let my short future fitly crown my past,
Resolute, sacrificial, till the last! " . . .

So the rude hills yet held him, now no more
   Going light of foot along their wavy ways,
Feebler of step while ever onward wore
   The hours of those inexorable days; —
Half glad to feel his futile searching cease,
Half eager for death's darkness and its peace.

Then it befell at last, one fatal morn,
   That after wakening he essayed to rise,
And moaning a great hollow moan forlorn,
   Sank backward with white lips and glassy eyes,
While round the rock-built vaultage where he lay
The careless dawn became the careless day.

Prone with exceeding faintness did he lie
  Till evening, and at evening was aware
That sounds of solemn storm were in the sky,
  And gusty spasms were shaking the dim air;
And while he listened his desire grew deep
Forth from the shadow-haunted cave to creep.

So, panting hard and straining his poor strength,
  He dragged his nerveless body pace by pace,
And under the dull windy heaven at length
  Crouched in the bleak light of an open place;
And then, while fierce gales tossed his whitened hair,
Girt with the growing storm, he prayed this prayer:

"Stern warders of the Flower, I charge you, hear!
  Witness, I charge, the death-damp on my brow!
I, impotent, that many a dauntless year
  Strode on through thorny failure, perish now!
And yet, imperious bafflers, while I die,
Even this deep thunder shall not drown my cry!

" For lo, I freight with fervor of appeal
  The black wings of the tempest! Lo, I make
These weak lips, that death seals with frigid seal,
  A voice above the rumbling cloud-heights wake!
By all my long hope's long unanswered need,
Spirits invisible, I charge you, heed!

" If yet she lives, that saintly and lovely soul
　　In whose dear service I have faltered not,
Attaining this my untriumphant goal
　　Here at the limit of my woful lot,
Grant me to find her feet, and kneeling tell
How mine fared faithful till the hour I fell!

" Grant me thus much, O ye that have denied
　　All else with changeless calm of disregard!
Yet deem not, thus demanding, that I chide
　　Your ways of hidden will, however hard,
Nor doubt remembrance of my toil has lent
Victory to mine hour of vanquishment!

" For though indeed this life shall straightway pass,
　　And the unborn morrow's first faint rosy ray
Shall find me dumb as granite on the grass,
　　While chance winds breathe above my pulseless clay,
This down-flung husk and sheath of what was I
Sepulchred only of the arching sky;

" Although, perchance, before a month shall end,
　　My naked bones lie pale, my body turn
Dust-booty for the frivolous gales to send
　　Anywhither, in antic unconcern;
Still, that I strove and faltered not, shall stand
Beyond the ruin of corruption's hand!" . . .

There through the strange tempestuous dusk rose high
   His fervent words till even the last was said. . . .
Then rolled the thunder, like a god's reply,
   Reverberate and voluminous overhead;
But ere the echo of the peal was done,
Turmoil and silence to his ears were one!

And while the strengthening storm-wrack's abrupt night
   Disfeatured all that mountainous domain,
Above him abject rioted the might
   Of ruffian blasts that whirled the sheeted rain;
And momently, unnoted of his eyes,
The lawless lightning rent the livid skies!

Long horribly raved the tempest, and long staid
   The startling interchange of peal and glare,
Till now, an utter stillness being made,
   No stem was stirred within the palsied air,
And dawn against the sky-line, dim to view,
Cinctured the opaque heaven with ghastly blue.

But broadening zenithward, the light began,
   As though some desolate polar sea should split
When Arctic summer cleaves its crystal span
   Of ice, disparting and dispelling it;
Even thus the darkness, to its core moon-ploughed,
Broke in great pearly bergs of drifting cloud.

And forthwith as the face of one who grieves
  By sudden joy is filled, its tears yet warm,
The lustre of innumerable leaves
  Laughed limitless below the wasted storm;
And many plaintive unseen insect things
Filled the wet world with dreamy murmurings.

Then wondrously he started up from swoon,
  He started with spread arms, and straightway knew
For true indeed the mild full-rounded moon,
  The scintillance of sward indeed for true!
And sure that no death-fancy tricked his sight,
Trembled in deep thanksgiving and delight.

Soon also, glad at heart, was he aware
  That all sore malady had slipt from him,
And that he stood on earth, with answered prayer,
  Potent in each resuscitated limb,
Still one in whom youth's fire hath ashes turned,
Yet strong to achieve that end for which he yearned.

While thus he paused, about the shining sward
  (For so it fell, as if by random chance),
Ere from those pale heights he went palace-ward,
  A moment wandered his half-heedless glance,
Beholding, severed by the late storm's power,
The ruined stalk of one wild mountain-flower.

And watchful of how low its leafage drooped,
  Compassionate regard illumed his eyes,
And close above the shattered Flower he stooped,
  Until his white beard touched it vapor-wise,
And on his hand one large tear, like a gem,
Dropt as he broke the green bud from the stem.

Then rising, with slow tremulous tones he said:
  "Be joined our sad fallen fortunes, fate with fate,
Poor bud, that in blast-levelled lowlihead
  Sorrowest for sweet hope unconsummate!
Surely with me 't were fitter thou shouldst fare,
Companioning with ruin my despair!

"We shall go down, we two, toward that dear land
  Whence in days distant my desire took wing,
And where like sea-foam to the sea-swept sand
  Manifold lovely memories yet cling!
We shall go down, while these calm hills, for us,
Abide indifferent to our exodus!

"Lo, here, in place of perished youth shall be
  The shadow of wrinkled age I am become!
And as I kneel upon allegiant knee
  To murmur of my life's long martyrdom,
Thou shalt well cast, poor bud of piteous blight,
Cold irony on that lost Flower's delight!

3

" But she, I doubt not, bending where I kneel
    Her sweet memorial charm of unchanged eyes,
Through all her soul's white chastity shall feel
    A new slow splendor of divine surprise,
Brimming it wholly, as pure dawn might brim
All a clean lily to the balmy rim!

" And then, I dare hope, dowered with gentle strength,
    Clear through my proud heart shall her vision go,
Until her spirit shall have learned at length
    The life-long fealty of my own to know, —
Viewed by one glad look, as mild lightnings view
Some deep cloud-cloister of the midnight blue!

" And though in that last hour we seem to meet,
    Given of the churlish years but slender grace,
As two that stand chasm-sundered while the fleet
    Immitigable dark hides face from face;
Yet in such hour, — nay, even at death's bleak edge,
To have deemed my stern past vain were sacrilege!" . . .

Down o'er the slopes of those dawn-lighted hills,
    Having so spoken, he set forth full soon,
By rocky barriers and by rainy rills
    And pines keen-pinnacled against the moon,
Or tracts of wood whose fissured foliage made
Pillared serenities of ghostly shade.

And marvellous also was the agile speed
   That spurred his steps on their steep downward way,
As though he had gained some grace of godlike heed
   That willed all weariness to stand at bay;
And he had crossed the utmost hill's lone height
Ere yet the suave moon held the central night.

Now onward with unlessening speed he went
   Over the lowlands, till three added hours
In distant fathoms of wan firmament
   Had reared before him the black palace-towers,
And reached at last the royal park, and stood
Among the bowers and aisles of its broad wood.

But when he neared the palace-walls, and let
   His glance roam as it listed, here and there,
Watching the parapet on parapet
   Of terraced lawn drop grandly through vague air,
The bloomful urns, the shrubs in gleaming line,
The carven cornice, the armorial sign,

Or yet the solemn portals of vast size,
   The graceful balconies vine-screened from sight,
The flickering fountains that curved petal-wise
   From calices of sculptured malachite,
The silvery pools, the slopes of dreamy fall,
The myriad-windowed palace proud o'er all, —

Now when he had viewed these fair shapes one by one,
  From time's tyrannic changes all seemed free,
As, after centuries of storm and sun,
  The immemorial dictatorial sea;
Nor could he mark a trace whereby to tell
Of the fierce years that plunder and dispel.

But when he reached the steps where grim in stone
  Two lions of mighty bulk were crouched at base,
Sheer from his jaded frame all zeal had flown,
  Craving for any rest in any place;
And forthwith, grown too tired to heed or care,
He sank in slumber on the stately stair. . . .

Then it befell for him that they who keep
  Ward o'er the weightless phantasms we name dreams,
Divided the dark tapestries of sleep
  On a drear vision of strange glooms and gleams, —
A glimmering cavern, huge and deadly still,
Like the cold hollowed heart of some great hill.

Rough-cloven of living rock the arched walls rose,
  In gray quiescence, in sepulchral light;
And here, while silence took intense repose,
  He moved with laggard steps, with doubtful sight,
And on through openings far away descried
New shadowy cavern into cavern glide.

But glancing earthward swiftly, in a trice
   He felt his brain reel hard in throes of dread,
Felt horror like a rigid hand of ice
   Assault his heart and make his limbs grow lead,
And strove to let one bitter cry cleave air,
But stood with locked lips and affrighted stare.

For all the cavern's amplitude of floor
   Was clogged with human forms whose every face
Death's pale indubitable sign upbore,
   Haggard and wide-eyed in that spectral place;
Yet though they seemed long dead, for some strange
     cause
Corruption marred them with no hideous flaws.

Then he was made aware, in this wild dream,
   That near him, risen from deeper deeps, there stood
Many commingled shapes of mien supreme,
   With beauty and awe to tell their brotherhood;
Shapes as funereal-hued and large as when
Thunder-clouds move in images of men.

But one rose kinglier than his kind, and he
   Spake presently, with rich voice pealing clear:
"Believe not thou the throngs that compass thee
   Allured but of their own blind rashness here!
Lo, these that sought the sacred Flower and gained
Void shadow, are thus defeated, thus disdained!"

So in his curious dream that spirit spake,
  Sweeping one haughty hand above the dead . . .
And now a silence which he dared not break
  Followed for many moments, till he said:
"And on my own life must the same doom fall,
Thus to lie lifeless in this monstrous hall?" . . .

Even then, as if for answer, he awoke
  Immediately; and now the morn was high,
And all the towering stair besieged of folk
  Who turned to him with many an eager eye;
And near him stood, both wondering hands outspread,
The King, deemed long ago among the dead! . . .

But when from prostrate posture he rose up,
  He wondered sharply that his hand should hold
A great flower, like a diamond-crusted cup,
  Dazzling with blended splendors manifold, —
A thing in truth so radiant that man's sight
Failed where it blazed, ineffable for light!

Lo, even to such magnificence of bloom
  Had burst the poor bud gathered by his hand
When pitiful of its vague moonlit gloom,
  Ere he went downward from that lofty land; —
Common and lonely then, but at this hour
Miraculously grown the long-sought Flower!

Nay, nor long sought! in truth, not sought so long,
  By many a fancied year, as he had deemed;
For now in centre of that marvelling throng
  Fair with all youthful majesty he seemed
As when he moved, ere yet the quest was old,
Lordly and lovely over wild and wold.

For thus far had the quest been real; but all
  Which followed by some wayward spell was lent,
Out from the dominance of whose dark thrall
  He woke at last in speechless wonderment,
Those latter years of weakness, woe and toil
Cast wholly from him, like a snake's dry coil!

And now, before another hour was fled,
  The King had learned the story of his quest,
And he had felt upon obeisant head
  The hands of royal benediction rest,
And heard the murmur: "Thou hast nobly won
The title of thy sovereign's chosen son!" . . .

So the King spake, with faint yet tender tone,
  As one that ill can hide besieging tears,
And left him in a great rich room alone,
  Those words like echoing music to his ears,
And all his soul like gladdened wine that keeps
A spear of sunlight in its ruby deeps!

But while he mused how fate had willed to send,
　　After continual sorrow bliss untold,
Softly was parted at the chamber's end
　　A crimson arras wrought with ferns of gold;
And issuing thence, with cheeks like rosy flame,
With eyes all starry fire, the Princess came.

And outward from no flower's fair covert slips
　　Any bright-belted bee its charms beguile,
Than brilliant now between flower-balmy lips
　　Broke the warm wordless welcome of her smile;
And watching her chaste face, for joy agleam,
It was with him as when we dream we dream.

Entranced, elated, thrilled, he faltered then,
　　While she drew nearer, clad in noiseless white:
"Not often, I think, does death so favor men
　　A moment ere his hand shall fall and smite.
Thou, beauteous Presence, wrought of shadowy dream,
Art not, for all thou dost so sweetly seem!

"Nay, I remember what the legends told, —
　　How, dying after years of empty quest,
Those other searchers would in dreams behold
　　The lost Flower's dazzling secret full-confessed.
But my lot verily hath larger bliss;
My death-dream wears diviner emphasis!" . . .

Then spake the Princess, murmuring: " Ah, be sure
   With all strange dreams and spells thy days are done,
Thou life no lustral fire might wash more pure,
   Thou valorous and unvanquishable one!
Rather than deem thou dreamest, meet at last
Me, the poor guerdon of thy laboring past!

"Ah, poor indeed! since how shall these eyes dare
   View shameless the calm grandeur of thine own?
Tried hast thou been by stern ordeal; but where
   Has my great worth at all been proven or shown?
Yet now, for nothing given, thy love is won, —
A gem outvaluing the vital sun!

" Pardon, if thy full story met my ear
   While mute I stood where yonder draperies fall,
Now quivering in thy presence to appear,
   Now motionless for deep amazement's thrall,
With rapturous thrills through my astonished heart
To see thee what thou so sublimely art!

" Ah, let my voice cry out, avowing all!
   Let me say fearlessly: ' I love, I love!'
Till memory, made obedient to my call,
   Comes phantom-footed at the sound thereof,
And lending thee one soft hand, one to me,
Goes down with us to where her dead years be!

" Art thou still mindful of the looks that met
    So oft yet transiently in other days,
Or of the sweet song thou didst rashly set
    Where I should ramble near it and should raise?
Yet couldst not thou, by vague and tender sign,
Judge of my spirit what I judged of thine?

" Knowing thee not, I knew thee!   Having heard
    Never thy voice, familiar seemed its tone!
Untold of how thy heart was ruled or stirred,
    Its lightest fear or fancy was mine own!
And powerless of thy love's depth even to guess,
For surety I believed it fathomless!

" And when, the palace through, thy wistful face
    In places where I passed was found no more,
I thought thee gone aloof to some still place
    And desolate, thy dark lot to deplore;
But of thy grief I did not dare believe,
Strong soul, how grandly thou hadst gone to grieve!"...

Then, ere the ending word of what she said,
    His arms had clasped her in impetuous way,
And two that loved were never lovelier wed
    By passionate human meeting than were they,
Whom now at last cold fate could no more part, —
Lips touching lips and heart laid warm to heart!

. . . . . .

Nor many a day had passed before the King
   Gave with high pomp of nuptials his fair child
To him on whom, for great accomplishing
   Through soilless worth of life, the people smiled,
And whose weird tale of quest from ear to ear
Had flown with wondering comments far and near.

And when at last the unsparing hand of death
   Bowed to his final sleep the monarch's head,
They reigned upon whose blended names no breath
   Calumnious or unkind was ever shed;
And always while they reigned the Flower staid bright,
Starring the crown with its keen peerless light!

But when that fateful term the years allot
   Befell this other King, mourned wide and well,
His wondrous Flower mysteriously was not,
   Vanished to nothing, as the old records tell . . .
Nor has its radiance once been seen since then
Through all new centuries by all mortal men!

BIGOTRY.

EACH morn the tire-maids come to robe their Queen,
   Who rises feeble, tottering, faded, gray.
Her dress must be of silver blent with green;
   At the least change her court would shriek dismay.

Each noon the wrinkled nobles, one by one,
   Group round her throne and low obeisance give.
Then all, in melancholy unison,
   Advise her by antique prerogative.

Reading the realm's laws, while they so advise,
   From scripts whose yellowed parchments crack with age
They bend the misty glimmer of bleared eyes
   To trace the text of many a crumbling page.

The poor tired Queen, in token of assent,
   At solemn intervals will smile or bow;
She learned how vain was royal argument,
   Back in her maidenhood, long years from now. . . .

Each evening, clad in samite faced with gold,
    The Queen upon her tarnished throne must wait,
While through her mouldering doorways, gaunt and old,
    Troop haggard-visaged crones, her dames of state.

She hears them while they mumble that or this,
    In courtly compliment exact and prim;
With shrivelled lips her shrivelled hand they kiss;
    They peer in her dim eyes with eyes more dim.

Each night the tire-maids lull her to repose
    With warped and rusty lutes whose charms are fled,
Till softly round her withered shape they close
    The dingy draperies of her spectral bed.

And so she wears the mockery of her crown
    With sad compliance, futile discontent,
And knows her people like herself crushed down
    By dreary tyrannies of precedent!

But sometimes, wakening out of nightmare's thrall,
    With clammy brow and limbs from terror weak,
Through the dense dark her voice will faintly call
    A name the laws have made it death to speak!

The name of one her girlish heart loved well,
  A strong grand youth who felt her soul's deep needs,
Who strove to snap her fetters and dispel
  The stagnant apathy of senseless creeds. . . .

Again from her steep towers, on that far morn,
  She marks him urge his followers to the fight;
She notes with silent pride what fiery scorn
  Leaps from his good blade, battling for the right.

She sees him dare his foes that swarm like bees,
  Brave, beautiful, a rebel, girt with hates. . . .
And now, in lurid memory, last she sees
  His bare skull whitening at her city gates!

SUGGESTIONS.

WHEN darkly o'er the mind have flown
    Bewildering mists of grief,
When doubt's rough arm has overthrown
    All bastions of belief,

When hope is like a flower that falls,
    Despoiled of bloom and balm, —
Even then we gain, at intervals,
    Majestic moods of calm.

Though empty looks the aim to explore,
    By words of mortal breath,
The mystery that is life — and more,
    The mystery that is death,

Yet gleams of happier change are known,
    Brief-clad with cogent power,
When feeling reigns on reason's throne,
    The sovereign of an hour!

And then, if so the heart shall choose,
　　Our thrilled and wondering sense
Can hear the voice of nature use
　　Aërial eloquence! . . .

When lonely memories of our loss,
　　In dreams to thrill the sight,
·Have swept funereally across
　　The draperies of the night,

Perchance, along the illumined land,
　　Dawn seems, with sweet release,
A white consolatory hand
　　That points to bournes of peace! . . .

Or if, when day is done, we pass
　　Where deep woods vaguely stir,
Whose branches hide the embowered grass
　　Of swards they sepulchre,

Perchance a sudden joy will greet
　　The breast that misery mars,
When clear through sundering leaves we meet
　　The high smile of the stars! . . .

Or yet the same rich pulse of thought
   May wake, in souls like these,
To watch the long pale pathways wrought
   By moons on summer seas! . . .

Or yet when fleet cool winds arise,
   At some harsh tempest's flight,
While half of heaven in blackness lies,
   And the other laughs in light! . . .

Thus many a grace through nature lives,
   By whose dear aid we gain
Some delicate sympathy that gives
   Nepenthes unto pain!

O soft appeals!   O shadowy spells!
   You seem, when earthward borne,
Like birds from far Hesperian dells
   In alien climes forlorn!

And whence you float, on transient wing,
   Ah, wherefore vainly guess?
Enough that while you bide you bring
   Sublime suggestiveness!

4

DESPOTISM.

NIGHT in Stamboul is at its drowsy noon;
   Like hollowed crystal beam the faint-starred skies;
Where cypresses throng black below the moon
   The pale domes of the Sultan's palace rise.

No sound this deep repose will break till dawn,
   Save when the tremor of some long breeze runs
Among the oleanders on the lawn,
   Where swarthy sentries loll beside their guns.

Dead still the town; close-guarded, here and there,
   The massive gates loom high in silver shade;
Alike o'er mosque and mart, o'er street and square,
   One silence of the sepulchre is laid.

Stern is the curse that crushes, bans or dooms
   All rebels that may venture, scheme or dare . . .
Some groan their hearts away in dungeon glooms,
   In exile or in slavery some despair.

What peace at last this Orient empire lulls,
  What safety from alarm its despot cheers,
Guarded by fortresses of human skulls
  That tower to-night o'er moats of blood and tears!

And he whose patient hope no peril dims,
  Whose desperate zeal no fear of failure mars,
To tear the chains from liberty's white limbs,
  Must fight his way through swarms of scimitars!

. . . And yet, even now, where purple pomps unfold,
  The Sultan, with all power at dark eclipse,
Dies from the poisoned wine whose cup of gold
  His own Sultana lifted to his lips!

A KIND OF PREACHER.

Volumes might be written on the impiety of the pious. — HERBERT SPENCER.

A MIGHTY moral teacher this,
      Who deals, with finely flourished arms,
Now in damnation, now in bliss,
      Now sweetly comforts, now alarms;
And skilled to clothe each view intense
With pulpit-shaking eloquence!

Nothing too vague or too sublime
      Transcends his confident surmise;
The awful ambuscades of time
      Conceal no secrets from his eyes;
The deeps of space he coolly sounds;
He gives eternity its bounds!

On nature's plan his looks are bent,
      And lo, she teems, we straightway learn,
With special providences meant
      For his rare wisdom to discern.
He scorns what science may disclose,
For she but talks of what she knows.

Poor science, holding in her hand
   A few scant remnants of earth's youth,
And having at her slight command
   Nothing more potent than the truth ! . . .
The sword of fact but ill appals
Where bigotry's great bludgeon falls !

He lifts aloft his pious gaze ;
   In holy wrath his features glow ;
For all dark sinning souls he prays ;
   His congregation weeps below.
He sees destruction's giddy brink
Thronged with these rogues who dare to think !

But once beneath his throne we sat ;
   We heard his discourse, word for word ;
And God was this, and God was that,
   And God was thus and thus, we heard ;
Till we, who merely mope and plod,
Envied this bosom-friend of God !

THE WORM.

WHERE garden pathways glimmer blithe
    And bees go singing, one by one,
I watch your clammy coldness writhe,
    In headless hatred of the sun.

Perchance with strange and mute appeal
    You question fate's capricious powers,
That harshly doom your frame to feel
    This long breeze trembling through the flowers,

Perchance you hold as dreary thrall
    This freedom, sweet with summer light,
And pine once more to loll and crawl
    In quietudes of earthy night.

Or yet, perchance, you loathe the dews
    That flash in brilliance here above,
But thrill to dream of how they ooze
    Through mouldy fathoms that you love.

THE WORM.

Or where the lilies break from soil,
  With taintless chalices of bloom,
Perchance you yearn to see them coil
  Damp snaky roots amid the gloom.

Ah, well! Few men with equal sight
  Can read the riddle of life's term,
And that which I may hail as light
  Looks darkness to my brother worm.

So, dismal burrower, hidden be
  Once more within your realm forlorn;
Grope dumbly down, and leave to me
  The balmy lilies bathed in morn!

IMPERFECTION.

WHENCE comes the old silent charm whose
    tender stress
  Has many a mother potently beguiled
To leave her rosier children and caress
  The white brow of the frail misshapen child?

Ah! whence the mightier charm that age by age
  Has lured so many a man, through spells unknown,
To serve for years, in reverent vassalage,
  A beauteous bosom and a heart of stone?

CHRIST.

A S one may watch the vapors die
   That shroud some greater star from sight,
Until its throbbing orb hangs white
In slumberous vaultages of sky, —
Even thus we watch retire and fly
   All shadowing mists of empty creeds
   That long have dimmed the immortal light
Of this man's golden words and deeds!

Man lofty and lone, yet Man no less,
   Though eager nature at his birth
   Had ampler dreams of human worth
To incite and thrill creativeness!
From awful urns beyond our guess
   Draining that power none plies but she,
   With holier elemental earth
She joined it, and the event was He!

Blameless, unique, he lived and spake,
 So wise above his lowlier kind
 That all the endowments of his mind
Seemed radiant as from godhood's wake.
He sought to quell the nameless ache
 That pierced humanity's heart; he sought
 Ease for its pagan thirst to find
At bounteous conduits of chaste thought!

He loved us in the o'erbrooding way
 That heaven bends over sea and land;
 The meek benignance of his hand
With sweet strange tyrannies could sway;
He bade us break the stubborn clay
 Whose bonds detain the ascendant soul
 From those pure summits which command
The glory and calm of self-control.

No prize beyond death his promise gave,
 No visible paradise of sense;
 He only implied that recompense
Which is to right, our side the grave,
As to the shaft the architrave, —
 That guerdon of sublime device,
 The realization high, intense,
Of individual sacrifice!

His teaching's rich remedial store
    Among unlettered listeners fell
    Not in cold idiom, as was well,
But soft pictorial metaphor;
Till they who marked its precious lore
    Thus blossom in parable or trope,
    Too credulously made it tell
    Illusory messages of hope!

What vital truths his counsel said
    Were called by supernatural names,
    Their grand utilitarian aims
Misvalued, misinterpreted.
His followers traced about his head
    The angelic nimbus, meekly worn, —
    While they contemptuous of such claims,
    Mocked him with fiery heathen scorn!

Fond ignorance, on his acts intent,
    Clad them in miracle's weird guise
    And linked them to the smart surprise
That dexterous juggleries invent;
Or yet fierce brains their efforts bent
    To assert him kinned with evil fates. . . .
    And so he moved before men's eyes,
    Half-cheered with loves, half-lashed with hates!

Girt thick by crime, yet free from flaw,
  Fearless he moved through field and mart,
  Philanthropy's divinest part
Substantiate in his life's pure law,
And showering on the world he saw
  Those peerless ethics, wide as air,
  Yet narrow as any hearer's heart
  For entrance and continuance there.

Then came the hour when scathed with jeers
  He fell before that last loud sin
  Whose echoing infamy has been
Vibrant through eighteen hundred years.
He lived pre-eminent above peers,
  He died with mercy in his last breath, —
  Yet only as gratitude could win
  Gethsemane, Calvary and death!

And since the Syrian sun looked down
  On that supreme historic woe, —
  The desecrated brow below
Its bloody and ignominious crown,
The stark nailed limbs, the ribald town,
  The insulting spear, too base to slay,—
  How many a creed has caught its glow
  From that one dire and lurid day!

What wild polemic heat has raged!
  How gibbet, stake and rack would fright
  Pale shuddering martyrs, morn and night!
And how, through centuries unassuaged,
Calamitous battle has been waged
  By hot ecclesiastic leagues,
  Till history's wan muse tires to write
  Of massacres, bigotries, intrigues!

And lo! this fury of sword and pen
  Was flung toward him whose love could span
  Humanity, and who pleaded man
For peace on earth, good will to men!
The reach of whose intuitive ken,
  Strong with desires to save and bless,
  Outsoared all philosophic plan
  In monumental kindliness!

But now at last through lovelier ways
  His bright identity may burn
  For the unfanatic few that turn
To watch it with impartial gaze.
Stript bare from fable's cheapening praise,
  A memory and a name unpriced,
  At last with reverence we discern
  The white humanitarian Christ!

THE DYING ARCHANGEL.

BEYOND the sense or dream we know as
      man's,
In heights or deeps where time and space are
      one
And either as the mote that specks a ray;
At fountain-head of mystery, force and rule
Whose funds of calm are causes of all worlds,
Ended, begun or yet to roll and shine, —
A being, a child of light and majesty,
Did evil, sinned a terrible sin, and felt
His immortality tremble, while a Voice
Whose mandate was creation and whose wrath
Extinction, spake the doom he feared must fall.

"So near wert thou to natal roots of good
That almost thou wert I, as I was thou;
And hence the incomparable deed devised
Of thee, sin's primal enemy, hath sent

A shudder among the voids where systems wheel
And made the soul of order rock with threat.
Great is thy sin, as thou, bright subaltern,
Art great; and therefore great must be thy shame.
Death is that shame; and yet a loftier death
Should take thee, as befits thy place and power.
So shall thy passing into emptiness
Be archangelic for its dignity,
As thou, archangel, shouldst in grandeur die."

Then he that heard with anguish, raised his eyes,
Dark as two seas in storm, yet dared not speak.
And while he stood, with glcry and ruin each
Blent in his mien, like some wild shattered cloud
That lightning rends and leaves, once more the Voice:

" Thou knowest of how among my million stars
One beautifully beamed for centuries, yet
Hath aged at last, and nears its fated close.
That star I love as I loved thee; for both
Served me in radiance as my vassals, both
Shone the exemplars of obedience, both
With memories of proud loyalty shall haunt
Eternity through all its domes and zones.
Go, therefore, thou, imperial in thy pain

Of exile and of punishment, to lay
The shadowed splendor of thy limbs and brows
Dying upon that dying star!   A world
Of melancholy as mighty as thine own
Shall compass thee, and while it fades and dims,
Thy spirit in unison shall wane.   Farewell!"

Then sought the Archangel, plaintless and alone,
This ancient star whose orb should be his tomb.
Once its wide continents had swarmed with man,
But now the torpid life of toad or worm
Reigned sole among nude fields and spectral woods.
No beast was left, no hint of leaf on bough,
No delicate wraith of flower, no glimpse of vine,
Or yet, through many a year, no trill of bird;
But all was dreariness and desuetude,
Fatigue, affliction, languor and decay!
The star had been a planet, allegiant
To a vast sun that glimmered at this hour
Wan as a wasted ember from its heaven.
In bends of rivers that had shrunk to streams,
On coasts of seas that flashed a glassy gray,
Phantoms of cities reared their roofs and towers,
With streets that swept by mouldering palaces,
With monstrous parks, where crumbling statues loomed,

With temples, mausoleums and monuments
In pathos of debasement; with long wharves
Where sick, monotonous ripples ever lapped
On towering hulls of rotted ships that once
Had scorned the ire of tempests, — nay, with all
To attest a race of such magnificence,
Dominion, empire and supremacy
As knowledge wed to wisdom nobly breeds.

Then, drooping low, the accursed Archangel spake:
"O star, I knew thee in thy luminous prime,
And loved thee not alone that thou wert fair,
But for the attainments and the victories
Wrought of thy peoples till they rose like gods!
For slowly did they climb, while æons passed,
From brutish aims to deeds of golden worth.
I watched and loved their leaders of high thought,
Their stealthy change of laws from vile to pure,
Their conquests over tyrannies and wrongs,
Their agonies, hopes, rebellions, and at last
The white dawn of their peace! But most of all
I loved, O star, the poets upon thy sphere,
And found in these melodious prophecy
Of dreams thy future waited to fulfil. . . .
But now thy future and thy past are one,

And I, who am fallen from immortality,
Shall rob thy dissolution, to my joy,
Of death's worst pang, being come to lay myself
In thee as in a sepulchre sublime ! "

So, while the dimness gathered gloom, and night
That had no morning shrouded these lone lands,
The Archangel bowed his head and screened his face,
And died in silence with the dying star !

TWO WORLDS.

A FIERY young world, in far voids of sky,
  Called to an old world growing dark and chill:
" Now that you near the hour when you must die,
  Tell me what mighty memories haunt you still ! "

Then from the old sad world this answer fell:
  " Vast peoples rose and vanished where I swing. . . .
But all my poor tired soul remembers well
  Are the great songs my poets used to sing ! "

WAR.

HOW long until the old sombre curse relent
    That shadows with its lurid pest our world, —
That often amid dismay and pain has hurled
The fairest isle, the mightiest continent?
    How soon shall all this power and reign of wrong
Back to a prisoning past be sternly sent,
Where ancient evils lie like serpents curled,
    Writhing with memories that they once were strong

Through ages glory about thy feet hath clung,
    War, terribler than all known shapes but they
    That deep in noisome charnels crumble away;
Yet proudly o'er thine hideous frame are flung
    To-day the purple and gold of kingly dress,
And round thee throng allegiant old and young,
    With banner and plume and pomp their love to pay,
    And kiss thy slaughterous hand's red ghastliness!

Thy smoking altars are the riot of strife;
    The great are of thy vassalage; alone
    Is he best loved that shall approach thy throne
Dripping most vilely with his brother's life;
        To restless monarchs' ears thy flatteries dread
    Thou bringest, pointing with ensanguined knife
    Toward fame, —a spire of insubstantial stone,
        That looms o'er glimmering meadows dark with dead!

The fumes of flaming city or village rise
    With welcome to thy nostrils, and the reek
    Of gore is delicate as no words may speak;
Thine ears drink greedily those tragic cries
        Of suppliant women seized in maddened flight;
    Vain prayers of the old for mercy dost thou prize,
    Or agony of the mother's thrilling shriek
        When her sweet babe is murdered in her sight!

And thou hast dared with ocean's loudest boom
    To match thy savage clamor, and to appall
    Its violence, when thy cannon's deadly ball
Rakes o'er blood-slippery decks a path of doom;
        Or when the lit wreck flares in hot distress;
    Or when the dim vast vessel, in midnight gloom,
    Suddenly at the sly torpedo's call
        Thunders and blazes into nothingness!

Or yet with exultation dost thou go,
  When truce its lull to battle and rapine brings,
  Where the sad hospital forlornly rings
With cries and moans of suffering, keen or low,
    And all the vacuous rant delirium saith;
  Or where at the ended fight's dumb overthrow
  Of man and steed, fly forth on massive wings
    The dolorous-throated poursuivants of death! . . .

Wisdom, thou lamp of nations, light supreme,
  With chaster brilliance glitter than of yore!
  Win men to seek thy beauty and to adore
Knowledge, whose rich oil feeds thy virgin beam,
    Till life to loftier longings be attuned,
  And from humanity, in both deed and dream,
  This folly of hate be exiled evermore,
    Now haunting it as foul flies haunt a wound!

O quench eternally these baleful fires!
  Wipe clean and sheathe henceforth from future ills
  This truculent sword that arrogantly spills
Fresh blood to hiss amid insatiate pyres!
    For lo! all thought where high ambitions dwell,
  All pure ideals of freedom, all desires
  Whose rush of godlier warmth man's bosom fills,
    Revolt from this black janizary of hell!

THE STARS.

BUSIED with earthly doings here below,
How careless of the grand stars do we grow!

How many a night while these most richly burn,
Toward all their flowers of fire we never turn! . . .

I dreamed of some strange world that cloaks of cloud
Ensheathed each evening in one dreary shroud.

Across the heaven at sunset it was drawn,
And wrought sepulchral darkness till the dawn.

But once, through each new century of that sphere,
The dense obscurity would disappear

And show the stars, for multitudes to mark,
Clustered and wreathed along the dizzy dark!

And then all tribes and nations, as they saw,
Would sink upon their knees in speechless awe!

POVERTY.

THEY that have borne such miseries yet endure;
   They that so often have cried are crying still;
We learn to name them lightly, these, our poor,
   As part of earth's irreparable ill.
   Us their sad voices have slight power to thrill,
      Their desolate haggard eyes but faintly grieve,
         Since we, who meet their anguish face to face,
      Through many a year its rigid truth receive
         As poverty's eternal commonplace!

All men, we muse, in shadow of trouble grope,
   Yet these are girt unchangeably from birth
With dubious gloom whereby the star of hope
   Shines vaguely on harsh crag or sinuous firth;
   Yet who may alter this unvarying dearth?
      Philosophy's astral splendors cannot light
         Cold want's disheartening dimness of eclipse,
      And science, although she weigh vast worlds in night,
         Brings no new morsel of bread to famished lips!

Famed thinkers, noble alike of brain and deed,
    Have grown white-haired in pondering how to give
These millions, bruised by poignant thorns of need,
    Some potent and benign alleviative.
    But still their burdening hardships grimly live;
        Still in the resonant city's careless heart,
            While deep groans pass on the wind like empty
                breath,
        Cadaverous throngs, mankind's far greater part,
            With rags for armor fight the assaults of death!

At toil they are stabbed with cold or scathed with heat;
    Tear-soaked, blood-stained, is the scant food they win;
From earliest youth round their unheeded feet
    Bloom tanglingly the red-flowered weeds of sin.
    Whatever bodily pain has worn them thin,
        Whatever sorrow has racked them, still they hear
            Starvation's rancorous wolves behind them press,
        While vice and ignorance, each with ghostly leer,
            Exult in mockery at their wretchedness.

Child after child, they are born to shame and woe,
    And stained at birth by even a mother's kiss, —
Too briefly pure, like those fair flakes of snow
    That fall amid the impure metropolis!
    What savage ineludible curse is this,

O sovereignty that rulest fate and time?
  Why are these countless lives thus blindly
    wrecked,
And made to dreary suffering or mad crime
  So terribly and so strangely pre-elect?

Age after age rolls onward; progress wheels
  Her golden chariot over shattered wrong;
Louder the limpid voice of liberty peals,
  Gladdening our world with archangelic song;
  Yet multitudes below the virulent thong
    Of this harsh doom go staggering to their graves
      With feet that falter and with shapes that writhe.
    O freedom, poverty has her droves of slaves;
      Thou holdest but humanity's mean tithe!

They suffer and die; they starve, burn, freeze and faint!
  We hug our treasures, and the old ill endures . . .
How long, O infinite God, ere this wild plaint
  Shall pierce the trance in which our spirit immures
  Its best nobility, and the " mine " and " yours "
    Clash with hate's fierce antithesis no more?
      How long ere love on a loveless world shall flow?
    How long, how long, ere we few, safe on shore,
      Fling spars to drowning myriads there below?

Have mercy, O men! O ye that strength possess,
  Bridge firm, with pity and charity for span,
The void of egotism, of selfishness,
    Whose gulf so sternly sunders man from man!
    Help with grand aid the unconsummated plan
      Of centuries moving to millennial goals!
      O seek that loftier grace, that richer good,
    That prouder patriotism, where earthly souls
    Meet mightily in sacred brotherhood!

FIAT JUSTITIA.

I.

THEY tell her he is dead; and when she hears
  Right instantly she fears
Lest they shall wonder that she sheds no tears.

"Poor widowed one," they whisper, for they see
  Her sorrowing mien; but she
Makes passionate inward murmur: "I am free!"

II.

She hears that he is dead; and when she hears,
  Leap the hot heavy tears
To eyes that have not wept for years and years.

And lo, she has forgiven him all the shame
  He wrought upon her name,
So blackening it with soilure of black blame.

Then to his home she hurries, yearning sore
  To look on him once more; . . .
But friends in awful virtue guard the door.

GREEK VINTAGE SONG.

I.

I WATCH the balmy moon of Crete
　Shine softly o'er the slumbering wheat;
I hear beyond the dusky firs
The silver flutes of vintagers;
I see the marble goddess gleam
Below the cypress, near the stream;
I wait, I yearn, I sigh for thee,
While vaguely calls the distant sea,
　　Pasiphaë, Pasiphaë!

II.

Aloof, in yonder breezy lawns,
Like some gay troop of graceful fawns,
With grape-leaves round their brows and throats,
The revelling shepherds urge their goats;
Or, with white robe and shining zone,
Gay Daphnis flies from Philemon . . .
Ah, come! I wait, I yearn for thee,
While faintly booms the mellow sea,
　　Pasiphaë, Pasiphaë!

NAPOLEON'S HEART.

" Imperial Cæsar, dead and turned to clay,
Might stop a hole to keep the wind away."

NAPOLEON in Saint Helena lay dead;
    And when the corpse had borne the embalmer's art,
A certain English doctor, it is said,
Placed in a silver basin by his bed
        The Emperor's heart.

At either side this precious thing he set
    An exorcising taper, slim and still;
And though he lay with eyes averted, yet
His curious charge he could but ill forget,
        And slumbered ill.

Now, after ugly dreams that shocked him sore,
    He woke at last to hear, when night was late,
A scrambling noise that loudened more and more,
A splash — and the dull falling to the floor
        Of a dead weight.

He leapt from bed and saw with wild surprise
   The vessel void, and overturned at that;
And saw as well, (could he believe his eyes?)
Dragging the heart along, in greedy wise,
    A monstrous rat!

The grim thief, once discovered, fled dismayed . . .
   And yet that heart whose vast dreams could control
Europe, and at whose pleasure thrones were swayed,
Just missed the ironic fate of being laid
    In a rat's hole!

ADAGIO.

WHEN memory is a harp in sorrow's hand,
　　How plaintive the æolian music swells,
As though a breeze from some enchanted land
Went sighing across long slopes of asphodels!

What pale wild spirits troop with ghostly tread,
When memory is a harp in sorrow's hand,
Funereal-vestured and rue-chapleted,
Gathering at her disconsolate command!

What wistful eyes amid that phantom band
Meet ours through portals of the unclosing years,
When memory is a harp in sorrow's hand,
To throb with melodies that are made from tears!

What spells of summons, while the deep strains roll,
Wake from its rest, with resurrection grand,
That shadowy Campo Santo called the soul,
When memory is a harp in sorrow's hand!

HABIT.

SHE marks the sure tides fall and flow,
   The white sails come, the white sails go.

Part of the shore she seems to be,
Like its old wreck, its one lean tree.

She knows not why her dim looks peer
From drab flat sand or headland sheer.

Her dress floats careless on the breeze;
Her face is wrinkled, like the sea's. . . .

'T was rumored once that in her breast
A small brown curl for years had rest,

And that when evening filled the sky
She kissed it and would say " Good-bye! "

So ran the tale, in idle way . . .
Her poor brown curl is lost to-day.

Perchance she seeks it, wandering so,
As white sails come, as white sails go.

But sometimes, while the sun drops down,
She takes a scrap of seaweed brown,

And looking at the far-off ships,
Holds *that* against her withered lips ! . . .

THE WISE PAGE.

THE brave lord, Baldwin de Poinceville,
    In his castle-court doth stand,
Helmeted, spurred and armed in steel,
    Ere he rides to the Holy Land.

His full grave brow hath a weary mark
    And his lips are drawn with pain,
As he stays his stately steed and dark
    By a touch on its jewelled rein.

And he whispers now, with a solemn care
    Lest his deep voice break for tears,
To the gentle page with the yellow hair,
    So wise beyond his years.

And he charges: "Be thou leal to serve
    Thy lady, the chaste and good;
Let not thy stanch young spirit swerve
    From seemliest vassalhood.

" Nor lightlier serve, for thy sweet part,
    Because thou long hast known
I cannot win her pure young heart
    To trust and love mine own."

" And bitter though the thought must be
    That she stands not here this day,
To pledge a parting cup with me
    And to speed me on my way,

" Still, guard her with proud zeal and glad,
    With homage that reveres,
As thou art loyal-souled, my lad,
    And wise beyond thy years ! " . . .

So charges Baldwin de Poinceville,
    And he sighs one sombre sigh.
But therewithal doth his young page kneel
    And with trembling tones reply:

" Heed me in this I do aver,
    Since I joy to swear it here :
With my zeal and homage both, sweet sir,
    Shall I guard thy lady dear ! " . . .

Away rides Baldwin de Poinceville,
   Stout knight, to the Holy War;
And the page to his lady's bower doth steal,
   And knocks at his lady's door.

" Open," he cries, " O my lady fair,
   And having no more sad fears,
Come, kiss your page with the yellow hair, —
   So wise beyond his years ! "